GREAT ANIMAL COMEBACKS
SAVING THE BALD EAGLE

by Karen Latchana Kenney

Ideas for Parents and Teachers

Pogo Books let children practice reading informational text while introducing them to nonfiction features such as headings, labels, sidebars, maps, and diagrams, as well as a table of contents, glossary, and index.

Carefully leveled text with a strong photo match offers early fluent readers the support they need to succeed.

Before Reading

- "Walk" through the book and point out the various nonfiction features. Ask the student what purpose each feature serves.
- Look at the glossary together. Read and discuss the words.

Read the Book

- Have the child read the book independently.
- Invite him or her to list questions that arise from reading.

After Reading

- Discuss the child's questions. Talk about how he or she might find answers to those questions.
- Prompt the child to think more. Ask: Bald eagles live near bodies of water. Do they live near you? Have you ever seen one?

Pogo Books are published by Jump!
5357 Penn Avenue South
Minneapolis, MN 55419
www.jumplibrary.com

Copyright © 2019 Jump!
International copyright reserved in all countries.
No part of this book may be reproduced in any form without written permission from the publisher.

Library of Congress Cataloging-in-Publication Data

Names: Kenney, Karen Latchana, author.
Title: Saving the bald eagle / by Karen Latchana Kenney.
Description: Pogo books edition. | Minneapolis, MN : Jump!, Inc., [2019]
Series: Great animal comebacks | Audience: Age 7-10.
Includes index.
Identifiers: LCCN 2018027584 (print)
LCCN 2018028147 (ebook)
ISBN 9781641282819 (ebook)
ISBN 9781641282802 (hardcover : alk. paper)
Subjects: LCSH: Bald eagle—Conservation—Juvenile literature.
Classification: LCC QL696.F32 (ebook) | LCC QL696.F32 K464 2019 (print) | DDC 598.9/43–dc23
LC record available at https://lccn.loc.gov/2018027584

Editor: Jenna Trnka
Designer: Anna Peterson

Photo Credits: Eric Isselee/Shutterstock, cover, 10; Ron Niebrugge/Alamy, 1; Phil Lowe/Shutterstock, 3; Shootnikonraw/Dreamstime, 4; viktor davare/Getty, 5; Topical Press Agency/Getty, 6-7; Gavin Baker Photography/Shutterstock, 8-9; Timothy Epp/Shutterstock, 11; Universal Art Archive/Alamy, 12; AP Images, 12-13; blickwinkel/Alamy, 14; Frans Lanting Studio/Alamy, 14-15; Virginia Department of Conservation and Recreation, 16-17; FloridaStock/Shutterstock, 18; PaulReevesPhotography/iStock, 19; moose henderson/iStock, 20-21; JustinLeeMedia/iStock, 23.

Printed in the United States of America at Corporate Graphics in North Mankato, Minnesota.

TABLE OF CONTENTS

CHAPTER 1
Eagles in Danger 4

CHAPTER 2
Protecting Eagles 10

CHAPTER 3
Wild Eagles 18

ACTIVITIES & TOOLS
Try This! 22
Glossary 23
Index 24
To Learn More 24

CHAPTER 1
EAGLES IN DANGER

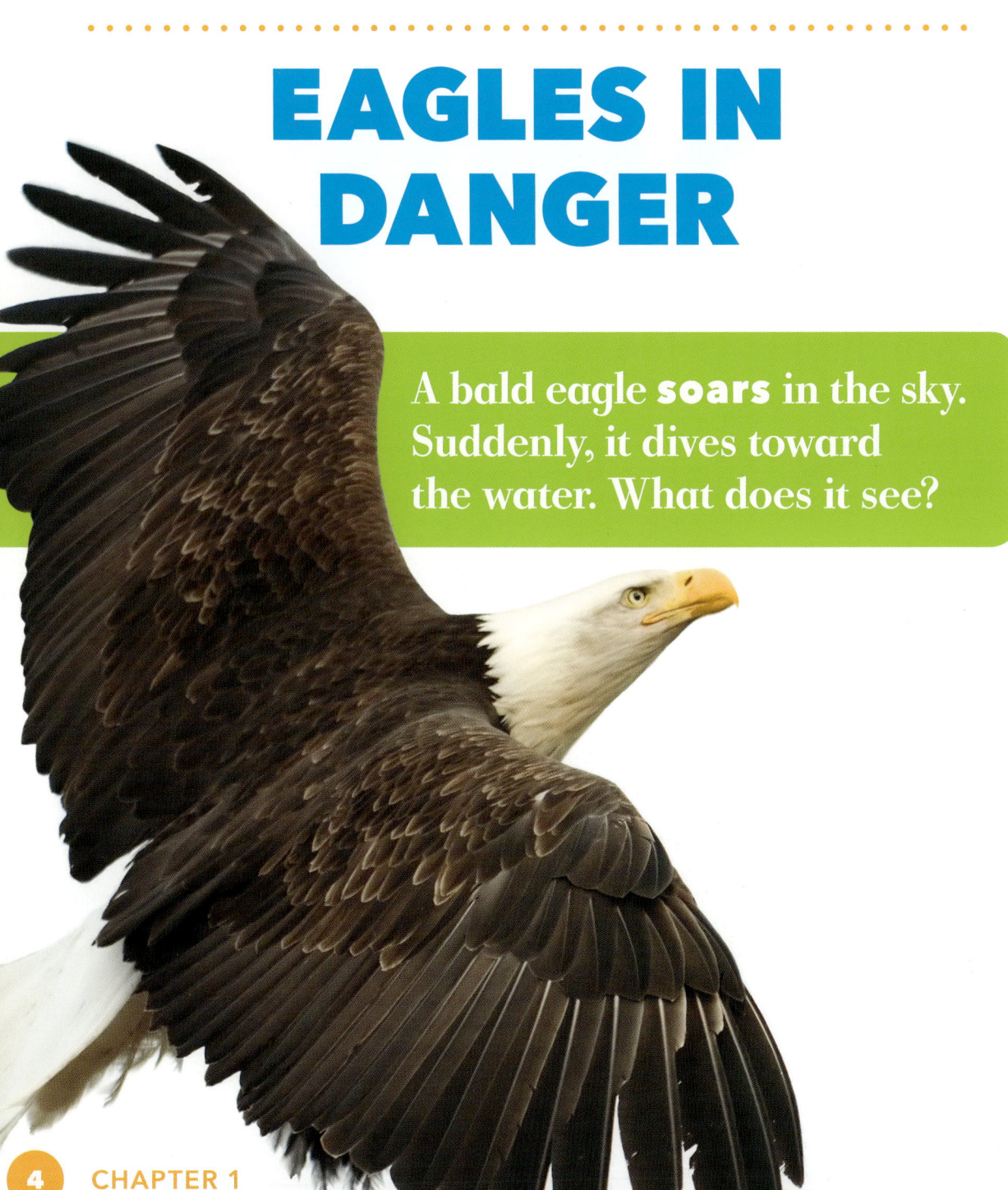

A bald eagle **soars** in the sky. Suddenly, it dives toward the water. What does it see?

talon

The eagle snatches up a fish with its sharp talons. Bald eagles once ruled the skies of North America. But they almost went **extinct**. Why?

CHAPTER 1   5

In the 1700s, there was believed to be around 500,000 **bald eagles**. Then **colonists** came. They took over eagle **habitats**. They shot eagles, too. Why? They thought eagles killed their **livestock**.

Even more were hunted in the early 1900s. The government paid hunters in Alaska for every bald eagle they killed.

DID YOU KNOW?

Bald eagles have amazing eyesight. They can spot a rabbit up to three miles (4.8 kilometers) away! How far is that? The length of 44 football fields!

CHAPTER 1

CHAPTER 1

In the 1940s, people started using a **pesticide**. Why? To kill insects that harmed **crops**. It was called DDT. It was sprayed on plants. DDT helped crops. But it got into rivers and lakes. It was in the fish that eagles ate.

The DDT made bird eggshells thin. They broke when adults sat on their eggs to keep them warm. The **chicks** inside died.

CHAPTER 1

CHAPTER 2
PROTECTING EAGLES

Bald eagles became hard to find in the wild. A law passed. It was called the Bald Eagle Protection Act. This made it illegal to kill or harm bald eagles or their eggs.

The law helped eagles. But it didn't protect their habitats. **Logging** cleared forests. Eagles were losing their nesting areas. Their numbers kept dropping.

CHAPTER 2

In 1962, a book came out. Rachel Carson wrote it. It was called *Silent Spring*. It told about DDT. More people learned how bad it was for birds like bald eagles. The book came out just in time. By 1963, less than 500 eagle pairs lived in the lower 48 states.

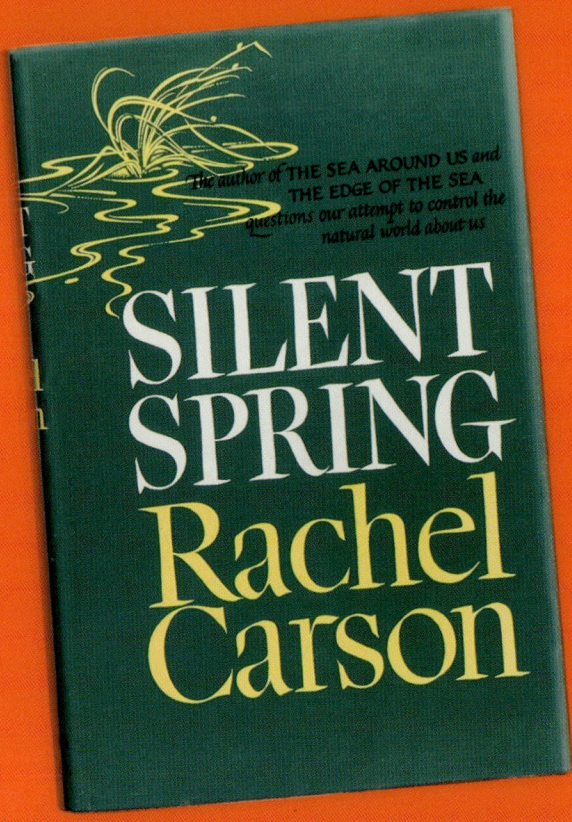

12 CHAPTER 2

Rachel Carson

CHAPTER 2

More laws soon passed. In 1967, the birds were listed as **endangered**. DDT was **banned** in 1972. Then in 1973, another law passed. The Endangered **Species** Act. It protected species close to extinction. Their habitats, too. The bald eagle was one of the first animals listed.

CHAPTER 2

The laws helped. Many eagles are now in **refuges**. People cannot build or live in these areas. **Breeding programs** help, too. People raise eagle chicks. Then they release them into the wild.

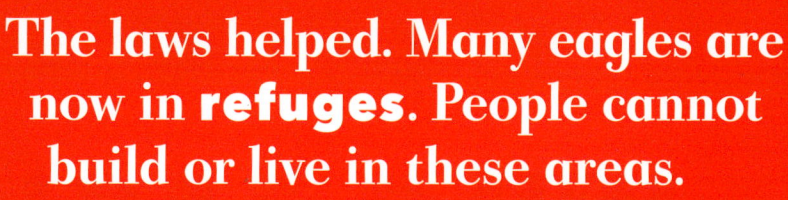

By 2007, close to 10,000 eagle pairs lived in the lower 48 states. They were taken off the endangered list that year. Now there are around 36,000 bald eagle pairs in the lower 48 states.

DID YOU KNOW?

Even more bald eagles live in Alaska. Roughly 35,000 pairs! Why? Few people live there.

CHAPTER 2   17

CHAPTER 3
WILD EAGLES

Today, bald eagles live across North America. Each one finds a **mate**. The pair stays together for life.

chick

Together, the pair makes a large nest from sticks. They build it in the tallest tree they find. Inside the nest are chicks. They grow white feathers on their heads and tails when they become adults. They can live 30 years or more.

CHAPTER 3 19

Laws and **conservation** helped bald eagles. They did not go extinct. But they still face dangers, such as habitat loss. Caring about bald eagles helped save them. With more care, they will continue to soar high in the skies.

TAKE A LOOK!

Bald eagles live only in North America. Take a look at their current range.

NORTH AMERICA

■ = bald eagle range

CHAPTER 3 21

ACTIVITIES & TOOLS

TRY THIS!

OBSERVING AN EAGLE NEST

Some eagle refuges put cameras in nests. Watch a bald eagle cam and observe the nest.

What You Need:
- computer
- notebook
- pen

❶ Ask an adult to help you find a bald eagle cam to watch online. Here are a few:
- Washington, DC, Bald Eagle Nest Cam: https://www.dceaglecam.org
- Decorah Eagles Live Cam: https://explore.org/livecams/birds/decorah-eagles
- Dollywood Bald Eagle Nest Cams: https://www.dweaglecams.org

❷ Watch the video for 10 minutes. Write down what you see in your notebook. Are there chicks in the nest? How many? What are they doing? Are the adults there? Draw pictures to show what you see.

❸ Visit the bald eagle cam once each day for a week. Write down what you see and draw pictures.

❹ Look back on your notes. Compare and contrast each day. Did anything change? Write a short paragraph about your observations.

GLOSSARY

banned: Officially forbade the use of.

breeding programs: Programs that keep animals or plants under controlled conditions so they can produce more and better quality offspring.

chicks: Newly hatched or very young birds.

colonists: European people who came to live in North America.

conservation: The protection of something, such as animals and wildlife.

crops: Plants grown for food.

endangered: In danger of becoming extinct.

extinct: No longer found alive.

habitats: The places and natural conditions in which animals or plants live.

livestock: Animals that are kept or raised on a farm or ranch.

logging: The act of cutting trees down for timber.

mate: The male or female partner of a pair of animals.

pesticide: A chemical that is used to kill pests, such as insects.

refuges: Protected places where hunting is not allowed and animals can live and breed safely.

soars: Flies or hovers in the air at a great height.

species: One of the groups into which similar animals and plants are divided.

ACTIVITIES & TOOLS 23

INDEX

Alaska 6, 17
Bald Eagle Protection Act 10
breeding programs 17
Carson, Rachel 12
chicks 9, 17, 19
colonists 6
conservation 20
DDT 9, 12, 14
eggshells 9
Endangered Species Act 14
extinct 5, 14, 20
eyesight 6
habitats 6, 11, 14, 20
hunters 6
logging 11
nest 11, 19
North America 5, 18, 21
pairs 12, 17, 18, 19
range 21
refuges 17
Silent Spring 12
talons 5

TO LEARN MORE

Finding more information is as easy as 1, 2, 3.

❶ Go to www.factsurfer.com
❷ Enter "savingthebaldeagle" into the search box.
❸ Click the "Surf" button to see a list of websites.